CHANGING the way WE THINK about PRIMARY MUSIC

CHANGING the way WE THINK about PRIMARY

Jenelle Allred

CFI
An imprint of Cedar Fort, Inc.
Springville, Utah

Paperback ISBN 13: 978-1-4621-4790-8
eBook ISBN 13: 978-1-4621-4841-7

Published by CFI, an imprint of Cedar Fort, Inc.
2373 W. 700 S., Suite 100, Springville, UT 84663
Distributed by Cedar Fort, Inc., www.cedarfort.com

Library of Congress Cataloging Number: 2024945688

Cover design by Shawnda Craig
Cover design © 2024 Cedar Fort, Inc.
Edited and Typeset by Sarina Betts

Printed in the United States of America

10 9 8 7 6 5 4 3 2 1

Printed on acid-free paper

DEDICATION

For the kids who feel they never get a turn.
For the choristers who are making the most of their turn.
For every music student I've ever had.
For the stake and ward primaries, orchestra, music camp, and private violin and viola students; thank you for giving me a turn.

Table of Contents

1
Introduction

You pull into the church parking lot Sunday morning and go for the best spot: the one closest to the door. Another car almost beats you there, and for a moment you both stay half-in and half-out of the desired spot. It's a stale mate, neither of you wanting to back down.

But then you glance at the other driver and recognition sets in. You see the crazed look in their eyes that comes from staying up until 2 a.m. the night before, see the self-paid and home-made stacks of posters and props that are shoved in their backseat.

That's when you realize. This spot? It isn't for you.

It's for the primary chorister.

You hurriedly pull away, not wanting the crazed look in their eyes to be targeted at you for one moment longer.

You say a quick prayer for that overworked, tired soul. Of course, the chorister in question has probably been praying for their soul since the day they were called.

The chorister feels the weight of being the main teacher and entertainer for all the sweet kids in your ward and often wonders if they are even doing a good job. But honestly, their biggest worry is that they aren't reaching the kids; that at the end of the day, the children won't feel the Spirit, learn the words to the songs, or enjoy their time in class.

So, what do they do? Every chorister approaches their calling differently. While some go in with a good outline, others struggle to plan lessons. Many dive into creative crafts and games that are fun, but have nothing to do with the gospel. Others throw song after song at the kids without explanation or connections.

If you are looking for a way for the kids to have fun while still making gospel connections, I'd like to propose a different way of looking at Primary music.

Ditch the stress of having the perfect-looking lesson, help the kids grow their testimonies through song, and create a class where the kids not only feel the Spirit, but can connect it to the principles they are learning.

This book teaches choristers how to refocus on the gospel and help kids build testimonies by doing three things: 1) Helping the kids connect to the message of the songs so that in times of hardship they can lean on the things they learned. 2) Providing the kids a simple, hands-on activity to help them engage with the gospel topics they are singing about. 3) Giving every single kid a chance to participate in the activity every single week.

I've had other choristers use some of my tips and lesson plans and also get great results. The following techniques may not work for everyone, but if they lower the stress level of even one chorister and focus their work on the gospel, then they have succeeded.

In this book we will discuss:

- The three goals of a successful singing time: testimony, connection, and participation.
- Making the gospel the focus of singing time and how to tweak those cutesy lessons we all love so that they testify of Christ.
- How to help kids connect to the music and use these songs as testimony building blocks.
- Ways to include every kid in every lesson.
- Giving the kids hands-on experience with the principles you're teaching.
- Tips for making lesson prep and teaching simple, along with lesson examples.

Is there such thing as a perfect primary music leader? No.

However, there is definitely such a thing as the perfect music leader for your primary. There are tons of music leaders out there with fantastic ideas, but you know what? They weren't called to teach music to the kids in your ward. Nope. You were the one called to teach music to the kids in your ward. With your prayers, your heart, and your talents (the ones you know about and the ones you don't), you can find a system and teaching technique that both you and the kids enjoy.

Just as there are no two identical testimonies, there are no two identical music leaders. You will be successful if you focus on helping the children to develop their own testimonies and connections to gospel music.

Want to have faith-filled lessons that are both fun and engaging? Then join me in the next chapter.

2
Getting Back to the Point

BEFORE I TELL YOU MY EPIC STRATEGY, I HAVE A FEW CONFESSIONS TO make. I have never used a flip chart. I know, scandalous. I've never cut off the bishop's tie, I've never played singing time measles, and I actually detest the popsicle stick system for choosing volunteers.

Now, before you think of me as a radical, I'd like to point out that I don't think these things are bad. In fact, some of my favorite music leaders use these tools all the time. So why don't I use these and other cute ideas? Two reasons. First, it's just not my style. It's ok to have your own unique approach to teaching primary music. You don't have to follow the popular trends or do what the last music leader did to be successful.

Second, cute things are only amazing if they add to the gospel learning and not take its place. Later on, I'll share some ideas on how to tweak those cute, tried-and-true lessons to testify of the gospel. I'll also share some of the activities I have done and examples of how to make the gospel the star of your lesson.

Every time you prepare a lesson that includes an activity, think to yourself: Why am I doing this particular activity? Is there a point to this? Will this activity be a good thing for the children in my ward? Will doing this help the kids to feel God's love or understand a part of His gospel?

I personally don't include anything in my singing time lessons if it doesn't a) have Gospel value or b) have musical value. I think there is definitely something to say about the value of fun. However, if all of your activities are purely for fun and don't have any gospel or musical value, then what is the point?

I'll give you a great example. There is a popular activity where the music leader brings up a kid to stir seemingly white powder into a glass of water. The kid is surprised when the water turns a different color. Whatever color it turns to then corresponds with a song that you'll sing next. On the one hand this is plain old fun, though it doesn't give very many volunteer opportunities, which I'll talk about in a moment. But does this activity have gospel or musical value? Maybe. You could argue that it helps you review the songs. But by itself, this is a fluff activity.

My suggestion is to transform lessons like the colorful water lesson into something that is not only fun, but can be an example of a gospel principle. For example, if I were to do this same lesson, I might do it while teaching a song about kindness or sharing testimonies. I would tell the children that sharing our testimonies can bring a special happiness to others and help them feel the love of our Savior. Stirring in the white powder would represent sharing our testimonies or being kind and the water turning an exciting color would show the effect that has on others. The experiment would hopefully take on deeper meaning for them. Same activity, different purpose.

Don't use up your precious time with anything you would classify as meaningless. Is it bad to do the colorful water activity? Absolutely not. But make a purposeful decision about how the activity will be used in your primary.

There are several fantastic ideas out there to help you come up with cute lesson plans if that is your personal interest. The kids often love these, and that's great. I'm not going to list these tried-and-true activities in this book, because a simple search for primary chorister social media pages will give you more than you could ever use. However, don't let cute lesson plans take the place of gospel learning. If you are teaching with fluff and ignoring the strong lessons you could be sharing with the primary kids, then you are missing an opportunity.

I've always approached primary this way, whether I was teaching in the classroom or being the chorister, but getting sent home from church during the COVID pandemic brought home the importance of using my time wisely. I remember panicking and thinking: What if I'm released before they let us come back to church? Will I feel like I've squandered my time or will I feel like I've done my best to share God's love with these little ones?

Ask yourself: If I have only one more week, one last chance to teach these kids something, what should it be? If I have just one opportunity to help them gain a stronger testimony, what should I do?

Make sure the activities you do have a point as strong as the songs you are teaching.

3
The Epic Strategy

WHENEVER I TEACH, I HAVE THREE GOALS: 1) HELP THE KIDS CONnect to the songs we are learning. 2) Give the kids a hands-on activity that will help them experience the gospel concept we are learning. 3) Give every single kid an opportunity to participate every single week.

These may sound like intense goals, but after a while they become second nature. Don't worry about the amount of preparation you think you'll have to do. With some lessons I prepared a ton; with others, I didn't really have to prepare at all. There are several example lesson plans at the end of this book that you can alter and use while you get the hang of it.

Goal Number One: Help the kids connect to the songs we are learning.

I don't want the kids to just learn the song, I want them to feel the song. I want them to think of the song lyrics when they are having a hard time and need support. I want them to remember that they are children of God and that their Heavenly Father loves them.

I try to help the kids connect by doing a hands-on activity and by sharing my testimony. Also, I let the kids share their own thoughts and testimonies when appropriate.

The point is to invite the Spirit into your lesson so that He can testify of what the song is teaching. I always say that I don't expect the kids to ever remember me when they grow older, but I do hope they'll remember the peaceful feelings we felt while singing these songs.

Some of the best ways I've found to help students connect to the music are:

1. Be earnest. Share your testimony. If you love a song, share that love.
2. Tell quick (30-second) stories that are appropriate for their age and testify of the subject.
3. Explain the song. Kids might not know what some of the religious jargon in the song means, you need to tell them so they know what they are singing about.
4. Teach prayerfully. Ask Heavenly Father what your class needs to know and learn from you.

Goal Number Two: Give the kids a hands-on activity that will help them experience the gospel concept we're learning.

This is one of my favorite parts of teaching primary. I love to think outside the box to come up with ways for kids to experience what I'd like them to learn from the music. If we are singing about God's love, I want them to feel God's love. If we are learning about how miraculous repentance can be, I want them to leave class feeling like they have seen that miracle themselves. The songs we are singing are testimony building blocks, and so any activities should be as well.

It should be noted that you don't have to do activities. This is singing time, after all, and the focus should always be on singing and testifying of the gospel. Remember that you are deciding what your own personal style of teaching should be, and activities, while great, don't have to look like any one specific thing. And, if you do activities, they should accentuate the songs you are singing and not steal the whole show. Singing time is for singing, so any activity should help strengthen the child's relationship with the song and the gospel. If you don't want to do activities then don't.

Most of my activities are designed so that we can be doing them while singing the song. I might teach the first line of song and then do the activity while we sing that line. Then we pause the activity and learn the second line. Then, while we sing the first and second lines we've learned, we do the next part of the activity. For the most part we are singing and doing an activity at the same time. This also allows the students to learn the songs well by singing the same parts over and over again without getting too bored.

For example, I had a box that I had wrapped in crazy amounts of wrapping tape (representing Satan's plan). The kids were challenged to unwrap the box while we were singing, so the box kept getting passed around to a new kid every time we sang.

In another one of the activities, we were trying to keep a kid's testimony balanced on "sand" while the "rains" kept tumbling down. Each child got a chance to have a turn to balance on the sand while we sang.

Whatever you think you know about singing time activities, broaden your horizons. Make each activity count. There are no fluff songs in primary, so there should be no fluff activities.

Tip: Remember that your lessons can be as easy or as complicated as you want them to be. There are examples of both types of lessons in this book, so take what you would like to incorporate and leave the rest behind.

Thinking up an activity could look something like this:

Step 1: What is the main concept you are trying to teach the kids?

I like to sum up the point of the lesson in one sentence. For example, say this week in the scriptures we are learning about how we can think of our trials as blessings and you want to tie that message into singing time by singing songs that support that topic. You could easily find songs that match this theme and sum up the lesson in one sentence: "I can turn my trials into blessings."

Step 2: What activity would be the ultimate experience for the kids to learn that concept?

If you had no restrictions on time, money, or reality, what activity would you choose? In the trials to blessings example, wouldn't it be amazing if we could all go on a trip back in time to watch Joseph turn his trials into blessings in ancient Egypt? Or wouldn't it be awesome if the kids could share their trials and have a blessing returned to them? Or wouldn't it be cool if we could somehow take a visual representation of a trial and morph it into something the kids recognize as a blessing?

Step 3: How can you simplify those ideas into something realistic that the kids would enjoy and that would help them connect to the song? This is where you take your big ideas from step two and scale them down. It might take some thought or research, but turning your big ideas into something realistic can create a really meaningful singing time.

In the case of turning trials into blessings, there was one week where I gave each kid a small piece of paper with a red frowny face on it. I then had them put the papers in my "trials to blessings bag" while we sang. Each kid was supposed to think of a trial that their frowny face represented. When the trials were all in the bag, I went back to the front of the room and—amazingly—pulled out smiley faces from the bag. The kids were astounded! I told them that through prayer, study, and asking Heavenly Father to help us see the blessings in our trials, we can see the good in the hard times around us and learn how to recognize our trials as blessings. More details on this lesson (and how I pulled it off) are found later in the book.

Goal number 3: Give every single kid an opportunity to participate every single week.

Yes, you read that right. Every kid, every week.

I am convinced that most primary music leaders don't remember what it's like to be a kid in primary and feel like you never get a turn.

Giving every kid a turn is a small, yet powerful tool to engage the entire primary. You want these kids to feel loved and needed.

This is a point I feel very strongly about. Why are we doing lessons or activities where only a fraction of the kids get to participate every week? If every kid in the primary is getting one to two turns a month tops, that is not enough.

Before you ask, I'm including large primaries in this. Having a big primary is no excuse for leaving kids out of the lesson. All of the lessons included in this book were done with an average of about 80 kids, between both Primary groups. Also, unless noted, all of the lessons in this book were done within twenty to twenty-five minutes at the most.

Now, you may have to redefine what a turn is. In the smiley face example above, I had a small piece of paper for every kid to put in the bag. That was the turn. You don't have to do huge things in order to give everyone the chance to feel involved. Just choose activities that are easy to use with multiple kids. Keep reading for more tips on giving every kid a turn.

As a music leader who has had her own kid in the class, I also wanted it clear that I was never favoring my own child. And yet, if every kid gets a turn, my kid will benefit from that system as well. If everyone always gets a turn, then everyone always has fun.

I had one caring and correct parent tell me that it was a good thing to not always give every kid a turn, that kids need to learn how to be told no and take turns. This is absolutely true. And, if your primary only gives a few kids a turn every week, I'm sure everything will turn out just fine. However, I felt it was important that every kid get a chance to participate in our hands-on gospel learning. I wanted every kid to experience these things, so why wouldn't I go out of my way to let them?

I'd like to note that even with planning to give everyone a turn, I don't call on children who are being irreverent. If they are irreverent for all of class, they will miss a turn.

Tip: Actions and music tools (such as egg shakers) can be fun, but they can also become a crutch when used too much. If you are only ever using things like this, you may quickly lose the attention of the older kids. As teachers, we can't gear everything toward the younger kids and then be surprised when the older kids aren't engaged.

How to Give Everyone a Turn

- A turn doesn't have to be some big production in which only a few kids in the primary will get to participate. It could be something as small as doing actions together, voting, asking kids to give their best emotional reaction, etc.

Depending on the songs we are learning, I often ask kids to "give me your best happy face," "give me your best shocked face," or "give me your best no way look." It's a way to get everyone engaged all at once. If I have the kids actually do something, everyone gets a turn. That doesn't mean that they get a turn doing the same thing, but they get a turn doing something.
Tip: Plan your lessons to include a type of participation that doesn't stress you out. If one of these suggestions sounds stressful, don't do it.

- Don't forget that small turns are important too.

I had one lesson where everyone got to throw paper balls at me (the balls represented hardship and sin). Everyone threw them all at once, trying to hit me and get around my literal CTR shield. Was having a shared turn a disappointment to the kids? Absolutely not. A turn doesn't have to be unique for it to be important. Everyone got to crumple up a slip of paper and choose which hardship it represented, which means everyone got to participate and have fun trying to hit me.

- Add a second opportunity for turns.

In one lesson, I had originally planned for the kids to help me with a single rain experiment that simulated trials. However, on further reflection, I realized that there was no way I would get all the kids to help me before class ended. To remedy this, I came up with a side project where some kids could have a turn decorating an umbrella with lesson-specific pictures, simulating protection from the rain/trials. (Note that all of these things happened while we were singing)

This sounds more complicated than it was. In the end, there was a colorful umbrella that lots of kids got to help with.

I won't lie, there were some kids that were disappointed that they only got to help with the umbrella. I tried to gently remind them that we were trying to give everyone a turn to help with at least one part of the lesson.

Was the umbrella as cool as the rain? Definitely not. But it was still a good example and visual aid to the kids of how we can protect ourselves from trials.

If you aren't a great multi-tasker, then this might not be the strategy for you. In that case, choose simpler activities that all of the kids can participate in without having a secondary activity for turns.

- The turn snowball effect.

Using the turn snowball effect is one of my best chorister tricks. Too often we get caught in a "one at a time" mentality, but where does that leave us? With maybe seven kids getting to have a turn each class? On a normal day teaching, this is unacceptable to me. The snowball effect is simple: start with one kid and then have them pass on whatever they are doing to someone that hasn't had a turn while you add yet another kid each round. (So the first round has one new participant, the second has three, the third has seven, etc.) You can do this with everything from using egg shakers to holding up pictures to drawing things on the board, etc. Before long, your entire primary will have had a turn.

- Have multiple kids go at once.

Most activities can be altered to accommodate multiple volunteers at once.

Example #1: We needed a lesson where our main focus was reviewing the songs for the primary program. I made a simple corn hole game using a cardboard fruit box and a plastic ball. The fruit box had several circles from where the fruit used to sit and I used a pen to write the names of the songs in each circle. Traditionally, with cornhole, you would give one person a turn to throw the ball. However, I had one person throw the ball and one person hold the fruit box, helping to catch the ball. And, just like that, two people get a turn instead of one. It was a silly, fun way to run the game. Note: This lesson had a secondary activity so that everyone got turns.

Example #2: In another lesson, I wanted volunteers to try and put together puzzles by the time the rest of the primary finished singing a song. I used simple blocks and taped a cut-up drawing of an ark onto them for one kid to do, I cut up a picture of Christ out of a magazine to use as another puzzle for another kid to do, and I cut up a picture of a CTR shield for someone else to finish. At first, I called up one kid for each puzzle. Then I called up two kids for each puzzle. Then I started bringing up three or four at a time. The extra kids were supposed to be able to help each other finish the puzzle in time. And, just like that, the whole primary got a turn and worked together to complete a goal.

- The turn avalanche.

This may sound insane, and it is, but at the end of class I usually bring up any kids that haven't had a turn so that they can participate. I have frequently had the kids line up next to me to be able to do this. Most of my lessons give everyone a turn early on, but sometimes they don't.

I did this once in a lesson by setting up a mini obstacle course. At the end of class, anyone who didn't get to run the course was invited to come up and run through (one right after the other) while we sang the song one last time.

Is this chaotic? Yes.

Is it worth it? Absolutely.

4
Tips for Teaching Music

Simplify Your Preparation

A QUICK WORD ABOUT PREPARATION. A LOT OF MUSIC LEADERS GET overwhelmed at the amount of preparation that goes into this calling. But don't let that sort of thing stress you out. Be happy with what you have the ability to plan.

May I remind you of the story of the widow's mite? Don't compare your widow's mite to a rich man's bank account. Your effort and donation is just as important, no matter what it looks like.

Utilize the skills and interests you are comfortable with. As you use techniques that bring you peace, your calling will simplify itself. For example, a lot of people use flip charts to help teach lyrics. I am not a huge fan of flip charts, so the thought of crafting multiple charts stresses me out. I would rather have the kids repeat after me or play a game to remember the lines to the songs.

If you like the idea of a specific lesson, but don't want to do the prep work for it, just figure out a way to simplify the lesson so that it works for you.

Use your talents and ditch the stress.

Be Prepared to Wing It

One time, during my missionary briefcase lesson (see the lesson examples), a little sunbeam came up to draw the missionary's face. He could do it however he wanted, and the face was dry-erase so it would only stay on his design for a couple of minutes. Halfway through the song we were singing, while he was supposed to be drawing, I noticed that the little boy was wiping tears from his eyes. I don't think any of the other teachers or leaders could see. Immediately I had to make a decision. What do I do? How do I handle this?

Easy. I let the other kids keep singing and focused on the one little boy. Going after the one sheep is what Jesus would do too, right? If he was getting emotional in his chair and me approaching him would draw unwanted attention to him, I might have let someone else step in. But he was standing at the front, under my watch, having a vulnerable moment. If it were my kid, I would want the chorister to be understanding and tender.

So, mid-song, I literally turned my back to the primary and knelt down next to the crying boy. He was so upset and kept telling me that he isn't any good at this, that he couldn't do it. He had drawn two lopsided circles for eyes and a little blob for a nose, and this poor little sunbeam was feeling like he wasn't up to snuff. This is the opposite of what that lesson was supposed to be about! I was wanting the kids to learn that their skills and blessings can help them be better missionaries, and here this little boy was sure that he didn't have enough talent.

I let him know that he was doing a great job, that I loved his drawing, and that it was going to look great on our missionary. When he persisted to despair, I asked if I could help him draw a mouth, because that would complete his awesome drawing! I guided his hand to draw a simple smile and then pat the little boy on the back, telling him that I was so happy with his missionary face and asking if I could put it up. I taped it to the missionary and the little boy went to sit in his seat, quickly calming down. He eventually smiled and I think he could finally see that his simple drawing did the job nicely.

All of this happened in the front of the room. It felt dramatic, sad, and a bit confusing. No one prepares choristers for these types of things, they just happen.

What happened to the rest of the primary kids while this was happening? Did they fall apart or all leave the church in an angry mob?

Did they lose their testimonies? Of course not. They sang half the song without me and we went on with the lesson.

Being able to wing it can be a great asset to your primary. I like to laugh at myself and remind the kids that mistakes happen and we just keep going. By dealing with matters on the fly, you can be an example of perseverance, peace, and faith that things will work out.

I want to be clear that handling things calmly does not always mean you feel calm, and sometimes I am not very good at practicing this principle. There have been one too many primary lessons in which I felt like a spastic wreck. I literally went home feeling like I was a good example of how not to act.

The times I felt like my mistakes or accidents were a blessing were the times I acknowledged them. For example, during one of my lessons I wanted each kid to come up to the front of the room where they would look at a picture of a very important person I had. When they came up, I would show them a mirror. The mirror was supposed to be kept a secret until all of the kids had a turn to look at it. Well, half way through senior primary, I asked everyone to raise their hands if they had not had a chance to look in the mirror.

I was so bummed. Here I had told all the kids to not tell their neighbors what they saw, and in the end I was the one who blew my own secret. I stood there for a second while all the kids, and teachers, started laughing at me. All in good fun, all in good fun.

But there I was, wondering how to salvage the rest of my lesson. So, in true theatric form, I ripped the blanket off the mirror and acted surprised. "Holy guacamole, it's a mirror!" Which of course got more laughs and we were able to continue on with the lesson, just in a different format with me being a little blunter about what we were learning about.

Another time, I had created cardboard trees to represent the sacred grove (don't overthink this, painting is an interest of mine so painting a few trees was nothing). I wanted to put them around the room on the walls, but that didn't work. So, I tried hanging the trees from the ceiling. I was amazed at how cool they looked, hovering in the front of the room.

When junior primary came in, I told them about my struggles I had experienced with getting the trees to the primary in the first place. But I reminded them that Joseph Smith experienced adversity in the grove, and he had faith to continue on and trust Heavenly Father. Just like Joseph Smith, we can persevere for good things. We began singing our songs in my makeshift grove.

Then the first tree fell. On top of me.

The kids burst out laughing, because, well, a tree just fell on me and I really hammed it up with a silly, shocked look on my face.

I could have laughed; I could have cried. I chose to laugh.

But then the next tree fell. And the next. It quickly became a running joke that we persevere, even when things feel like they are falling down around you.

By the end of junior primary, most of the trees had fallen down. Fortunately, the kids got a kick out of it and the troubles made my lesson all the better.

Feel Free to Frustrate the Kids

Some of my best lessons were the ones where I frustrated the kids or got them to argue with me. For example, in one of my lessons I wanted the kids to realize that hardship is part of life. That week in the scriptures we had studied about how hardships can be blessings. So, I set up a game day where we would play different games while singing. Only, I rigged all of the games so that you couldn't lose them. I taped the eggs to the spoons and pre-pinned the tail on the donkey. That sort of thing. The kids quickly got the point that without the ability to lose, all of these games were lame! And boy did they let me know it. By the end of the lesson, they were so mad. One kid let me know about his displeasure when I took out the doughnut-on-a-string eating contest where all the doughnuts were already eaten so that no one would lose! He was not the least bit happy about that.

But the setting was perfect! I was able to say a few words to the angry primary that went something like this:

Hey! Wait a minute, wait a minute. Are you telling me that you'd rather have real games? Games that are hard? Games where you can make mistakes and sometimes fail? Wait a minute, wait a minute. Are you telling me that things in life are better when you actually have to show some hard work?

The answer was a resounding yes.

If you can get the kids to teach you the lesson, you've succeeded.

Stay Focused on What Is Important

All it takes is one conversation with another music leader, let alone a whole social media group full of them, to suddenly feel like your humble offering is not enough. Instead of realizing you've been called to teach the gospel through music, you feel as though you've been called to recreate a blog-worthy lesson every single week just to teach a song.

There are fewer ways to strike fear in the heart of a church member than by saying the words, "We'd like to call you to be the primary music chorister." Being in charge of all the young kids in the ward and singlehandedly keeping their attention? What kind of sweet torture is this, you ask.

By the time people start telling you funky ways to quiet the kids down and how to get flip charts printed on the cheap, you've really begun panicking. Why, Oh Lord, have you chosen to put this trial on me?

Maybe you feel like a glorified babysitter. "If I can only keep the kids interested long enough to get them out of my hair, then all is well." Or maybe you're the opposite. Maybe you're like me and love teaching primary music. Dare I say that even those who enjoy this calling are not impervious to the crushing questions: Will the kids like me? What if they find my teaching style boring?

And then there are those that have completely forgotten what this calling is really about. They've fallen into the craft-trap and they can't escape the panic unless they've created a lesson that is literally picture-perfect.

Part of why I wrote this book is to help reset these invasive mindsets that have cemented their way into those of us with this calling.

Strip the calling down to the basics, and what do you get? Teaching the gospel through song. Sharing your testimony.

The lesson examples at the end of this book can be used to give you ideas in crafting the best type of lessons to help the kids actively participate in learning the songs and growing their testimonies. But don't forget that your teaching style, your own testimony, is what is truly and deeply important for the kids to learn.

These examples are purely to give you an idea of how to implement the principles from this book. The topic of your lessons will ideally fit with what was studied that week.

Stand strong. You are not just a chorister; you are a child of God. We are growing testimonies, not professional singers. You've got this!

5
Planning the Primary Program

The primary program is often one of the highlights of the year. It has the power to turn frowns upside down and bring tears to the eye. The program can soften hearts and teach the gospel to those visitors that may not otherwise hear it.

So, should you be stressing about the primary program? No! The program is simply a chance for the kids to share what they've been learning.

If you find yourself worrying about how to structure or run your program, remember three things:

1. Every primary plans their program differently. You don't have to make your program just like everyone else's.
2. There have been many programs before yours and there will be many programs after. If you have never planned a program, there's a good chance you've watched one (or dozens) of them throughout your life. Just by thinking through what you've witnessed, you could probably plan a simple primary program in under an hour. If you have never seen a program before, don't sweat it. Keep reading the rest of this section and ask the other adults in the primary for help. You've got this.
3. As long as you invite the Spirit, everything else will work itself out.

Primary programs, like weekly singing times, are excellent opportunities for the kids to grow their testimonies and engage with the gospel. There are several ways to help each kid feel the Spirit and be engaged, but first let's talk about designing a basic primary program.

1. Choose your songs.

You can learn songs especially for the primary program, but you can also take the songs you've been learning throughout the year and decide which order you'd like to sing them in the program. I'd suggest mixing up the song order so that the songs vary in length, difficulty, and speed. For example, if you have three songs that are simple and short, the kinds of songs that are picked up quickly by students, I would space them out between the longer, harder songs. In doing this you avoid a situation where all the easy songs are sung at once, leaving the young and struggling kids bored or extra nervous the rest of the time because they don't know the more difficult songs.

Also, consider what it is like for the audience when listening to the songs. Making sure you don't have multiple slow songs in a row will help your audience stay awake.

Tip: If your primary is small and nervous to sing or the kids are struggling with the songs, consider asking the congregation to sing along.

2. Decide if you want the kids to have speaking parts.

There are several ways to do speaking parts in a primary program. I've seen programs where only a few kids or the oldest kids have speaking parts, others where kids from the older class sit with one of the younger classes and lead them up between songs to say their parts, others where the kids answer a question, and others where the kids have a script of what to say.

I love hearing personalized talking parts from each of the children. Letting them create their own answers to a common question gives the kids an opportunity to internalize the gospel topic. On the other hand, assigning written parts or scriptures helps them learn as well. Primaries that are small can let the kids say more or give a talk because they will have more time. Sometimes the primary president or bishop will speak or bare their testimony, sometimes they won't. Families can assist when needed.

For an easy way to assign speaking parts, switch off between songs and speaking parts and assign each class a question based on the song you are about to sing. For example, if you are about to sing a song about Christ, you could have the kids each finish the following sentence: My favorite story about Christ is when He _________. If you are singing a song about service, you can have the kids share their favorite kind of service to give. Going down your list of songs, come up with a simple question that goes with each one, and just like that your basic primary program is complete.

Tip: Make planning easier by letting class teachers help with the speaking parts. You can tell a class that they are assigned a question and then let them talk about it in class. Teachers can write down the answers that the kids want to give so that if they need a reminder on the big day then you have a list of the answers. There are several ways to remind the kids of their answers. A member of the presidency can sit by the microphone, teachers can go up with their class and help any struggling kids, or students from an older class can help the younger ones know what to say.

Tip: It's smart to have teachers or presidency members on the stand with the kids to help with emotional support and remind them to be reverent when needed. It's also smart to thank your teachers for doing this since most of them won't want to.

3. Decide how you want the kids arranged on the stand.

The layout of the chapel or room will change how you want the kids to be arranged. For small primaries, the existing chairs may be enough. For larger primaries, using the floor in front of the pulpit for them to stand may be needed. I've also seen some primaries use platforms in front of the pulpit for kids to sit on or reserve the front rows of the chapel for kids to sit on and then stand up and turn around when it is time to sing.

These are the basics of a primary program, but there are several other ways you can use the program as a testimony builder.

Here are some tips for getting the most out of your primary program:

- Choristers: Follow the direction of the presidency.
  Presidencies: Follow the direction of the chorister.

It's important for the presidency and chorister to work together. If you are the chorister, remember that the presidency is over the entire primary. If you are in the presidency, remember that the chorister has been called to be the teacher during singing time. If either the chorister or the presidency feels steam-rolled over and ignored then something needs to change. You can't work independent of each other. Go by the handbook.

- The program: an opportunity to grow testimonies.

The three goals of a successful singing time can help lead to a successful primary program. If you are helping the kids to connect to the songs, experience the gospel topics, and stay engaged, then what they have learned will show in their singing. When considering what to do for speaking parts, choose something that will help the kids grow and internalize the topics studied.

- Practice Incentives

For added fun in practicing, some choristers create charts or some other visual display to help the kids get excited for their program and to show how well they have prepared a certain song. For example, the chart might have different levels of proficiency and each week the song can be updated. Sort of like a game board where every step you make takes you closer to the finish line. The finish line can simply be "ready to sing" or it can be a special treat, like "cookies" to be eaten after the primary program or at a practice.

- Practice Opportunities

Primaries will often get together for an extra practice outside of normal church hours. This may take place on a weekday or a Saturday. Make sure to not overdo practices. The primary program is to showcase what we have been learning this year, not to make sure the kids are classically trained vocalists. Any extra practice should still be reverent and fun, and should probably end with a treat.

Sometimes primaries will practice in the chapel if it is available during primary hour. When you get together, make sure to have the kids practice:

- The songs and spoken parts in the order they are supposed to happen.
- How to walk from their seats to the pulpit and back to their seats again.
- How to be reverent and good examples when seated on the stand.
- How to follow your cues for when to stand and sit.

During the program and practices, it is helpful if every adult involved (on the stage and running the program) has a copy of the program's song and speaking part order. That way everyone can follow along and know exactly when it is their turn to do something.

- Including every kid in the primary program:

I love including every kid in every primary activity, and the primary program is no exception. With a big primary, giving everyone a small question to answer or part to read is easy. You could also include their families or the congregation if you have a small primary and need some help. Here are some ways, on top of singing and speaking parts, that you could include every kid in the program:

- Instrumental Pieces

One of my favorite primary memories is asking a bunch of kids if anyone plays an instrument and wants to do a combined number for the primary program. Several kids raised their hand and I was so excited. I went through one by one, and aside from several piano players and two violinists, I got some funny answers. One kid thought that playing video games counted as playing an instrument.

Having the two violinists play something together was easy. The harder task was trying to include ten or so young pianists in the program. What we ended up doing was inviting them to play the prelude music. Timing was first come first serve, and the idea was that the pianists could rotate playing one song at a time until the meeting started. It ended up being fantastic and it didn't matter how advanced they were. Whether it is a group of primary students or a family that participates, musical numbers are fun and can invite the Spirit.

- Printed Programs

One of the cutest things I've ever seen is when a primary colored the covers of the printed programs for stake conference. I remember thinking, someone should do this for the primary program! Having the kids color a black and white program is an easy way to get them all involved and feel like they were part of making the magic happen.

- More ideas for kids who don't want to participate...

If a kid doesn't want to speak or even get up on the stand, don't force them or make them feel guilty.

For these kids, offering other opportunities to help might be appreciated. If a kid doesn't want to participate because they feel too old to sing, you could ask them to help hand out printed programs or show people a QR code to download it.

You could ask a nervous kid to sit by you and help hold up signs that say what song you are about to sing. If a kid wants to sing but they don't want to be up on the stand, you could ask them to sit next to you or in front of the younger kids and be an example of reverence while they sing (folded arms, being quiet, etc.)

If it would freak out a kid to help at all, then don't push it. However, if the kid would enjoy having another way to help, then it could be a good idea to talk to their parents and see what they think.

6
Lessons at a Glance

THIS SECTION HAS BRIEF SUMMARIES OF LESSON IDEAS YOU COULD use. The full lessons can be found in the next chapter.

Lesson: The Protection of Choosing the Right.

Purpose: Choosing the right can help us withstand hardship.

In this lesson, each kid gets their own half piece of paper to crumple up and throw at the teacher, who is hiding behind a massive CTR shield. Each kid chooses what hardship or trial their paper represents. Hardship and trials attack the teacher, but he or she is able to better withstand the attack because of the shield. The teacher then takes a turn holding up a tiny CTR shield (not choosing the right as much) and discovers that it won't protect as well when the kids throw their trials. Commit to choosing the right all the time, not just a little. For more information, visit page 33.

Lesson: Primary Musical!

Purpose: Connect primary songs to principles in a scripture story.

In this lesson you put on a mini play to teach the kids a scripture story through the use of primary music. Children take turns briefly standing in for characters in the play. This is a great low-prep lesson, which can also be high-prep if you want to bring props. For more information, visit page 35.

Lesson: The Crown of a Child of God

Purpose: We can choose the right and recognize our blessings from being children of God

In this lesson, the kids help make a child of God crown for the teacher to show our royal heritage. Each part of the crown represents a different blessing or gift that we get as children of God, as well as good choices we can make. As the crown gets taller, the fun begins. For more information, visit page 37.

Lesson: Be Bold in Following Christ.

Purpose: We can follow Christ despite opposition.

In this lesson you use "call to action" songs to teach the kids about a scripture story that reminds them they can be bold in following Christ, despite the opposition and trials that try to get in their way. As you tell the scripture story, you sing the bold songs. For more information, visit page 39.

Lesson: I Can Build an Ark by Choosing the Right.

Purpose: We can build an ark of spiritual safety by making good choices.

In this lesson the children build an ark with "planks" that represent good choices. For more information, visit page 40.

Lesson: Being Able to Choose Is a Blessing.

Purpose: It is a blessing to be able to choose the right because of Christ's plan.

In this lesson, the kids get to work on a puzzle that represents Satan's plan (all the puzzle pieces are the same boring square, there is no personal choice involved and it doesn't matter where you put the pieces). After the primary realizes how boring it is to not get to choose or work with puzzle pieces that are individualized, you put together a puzzle that represents Christ's plan. For example, a picture of a temple or Christ. For more information, visit page 42.

Lesson: Faith Is like a Little Seed.

Purpose: Inspiration for testimonies can come in all sizes, both small and large.

In this lesson, you compare different sizes of seeds from around the world and talk about different types of sources for building testimony. The kids will enjoy talking about the tiniest seeds on the planet, as well as helping to lift up folding chairs to represent the weights of huge seeds. This lesson takes very little preparation. For more information, visit page 44.

Lesson: Song Toolbox

Purpose: Church songs can be used to help comfort and strengthen us.

In this lesson, the kids choose different songs from a toolbox. As we sing the songs, we also talk about how we can use that song to help us in our lives. For more information, visit page 46.

Lesson: I Am like a Star.

Purpose: Every single one of us is important and needed in the kingdom of God.

In this lesson the kids put on a light show and learn that we are each important to God. This lesson has several ideas that can be broken up to create multiple lessons if needed. One part of the lesson that uses a strand of Christmas lights is super easy and can be prepared last minute if needed. For more information, visit page 47.

Lesson: Stand in Holy Places

Purpose: Choosing the right places to be can protect us and help us through trials.

In this lesson we do an experiment with a small rain simulator and a toy man. Unless the man is standing under the CTR umbrella, he gets soaked. He will still get wet/experience trials under the umbrella, but not as much as if he doesn't "CTR" at all. For more information, visit page 50.

Lesson: We Can Get Blessings from Our Trials.

Purpose: Trials, or how we view our trials, can turn into blessings.

In this lesson, we turn trials into blessings. Each kid gets to put a small red frowny face into a brown paper "trials to blessings bag." Each kid chooses what trial their frowny face represents. Then, through an easy magic trick, the teacher pulls the slips of paper out of the bag and they are surprisingly green smiley faces, otherwise known as blessings. For more information, visit page 54.

Lesson: Missionary Briefcase

Purpose: Every kid can become a good missionary.

In this lesson, the teacher turns a whiteboard into a missionary's briefcase. Kids take turns coming up to draw something that represents their talents or good choices they can make. This is so kids can connect their own talents and choices to how they might be a good missionary. For more information, visit page 56.

Lesson: We Are Part of God's Army.

Purpose: We can stand with God no matter what obstacles are in our way.

In this lesson, the kids complete a miniature obstacle course while in "basic training" for God's army. For more information, visit page 58.

Lesson: Pioneers Worked Hard and Played Hard.

Purpose: We can learn from the Pioneer's hope and work ethic.

In this lesson, the primary room is transformed into a pioneer wagon train where the kids get to work, eat, and play like pioneers. This is a slight twist on a typical Pioneer Day singing time lesson. For more information, visit page 59.

Lesson: The Holy Ghost Speaks to Us in Different Ways.

Purpose: We can learn how the Holy Ghost speaks to us individually.

In this lesson we learn about the different ways to feel the Spirit and how it can be a unique experience for everyone. The kids come up with actions to represent the different ways while we sing. For more information, visit page 61.

Lesson: Tell a Story

Purpose: Certain songs are sung as a story.

In this lesson we take a song that is told in story format and let the kids tell the story through pictures while we sing the song. For more information, visit page 62.

Lesson: Following

Purpose: We can learn to follow Jesus Christ and the prophet.

In this lesson the kids practice their following skills. This lesson needs no prep. For more information, visit page 63.

Lesson: He Lives.

Purpose: The tomb is empty because Christ lives.

In this lesson the kids empty a "tomb" of pictures of Christ and create a collage. Each picture taken out has the next line of the song on it. This is supposed to be a very reverent lesson. For more information, visit page 64.

Lesson: The Auto-Husband 3000 (Father's Day; Can be Adjusted for Mother's Day)

Purpose: Good choices help men to be good husbands and fathers.

In this lesson the kids help build a husband/father out of special attributes and good choices that help men be good husbands and fathers. This lesson can be used for Mother's Day as well, with a few slight adjustments. For more information, visit page 65.

Lesson: The Magic of Repentance

Purpose: Through the atonement of Christ we can repent and become clean.

In this lesson, the teacher does a magic trick that can turn a sad, sin-filled picture into a happy picture of a person making good choices. For more information, visit page 67.

Lesson: Breaking Down a Song.

Purpose: We can gain a deep understanding of each song.

In this lesson, the teacher explains the importance of each line of the song. While it is good to do this anyway, this particular lesson explains the song in depth while still making the lesson interesting. For more information, visit page 68.

Lesson: Am I a Child of God?

Purpose: We are all children of God.

In this lesson, the teachers and students are reminded that everyone is a child of God. This is also a good get-to-know-you lesson. For more information, visit page 71.

Lesson: Don't Forget to Pray.

Purpose: Heavenly Father is just a prayer away.

In this lesson, the teachers and students do everything to open up a sealed box except actually lift off the lid. By the end of the lesson the kids will be so frustrated that the teacher isn't doing the obvious choice to get into the box. When the class finally does lift the lid, they find a picture of God. Sometimes we forget that prayer is a simple, direct connection to God. Don't dance around the box, lift the lid. For more information, visit page 72.

7
Lessons In-depth

Lesson: The Protection of Choosing the Right.

Purpose: Choosing the right can help us withstand hardship.
Pairs well with songs that discuss faith, choosing the right, or following the prophet.

Materials:

- A large CTR shield
- A ridiculously tiny CTR shield
- Paper

I started my lesson with an awesome, battle-worn CTR shield that I'd made out of cardboard. It was huge, with plenty of room for me to hide behind. I acted like a warrior, really hamming it up. I asked the kids if they thought choosing the right would protect me from hardships and sin.

I told them that choosing the right will help protect you from sin, but it won't stop hardships or sadness from coming into your life. However, choosing the right will help you be able to handle those hardships because you'll have the peace of knowing you are making good choices.

I used the story of Noah as an example. Choosing the right and following God literally protected him and his family from the flood. They still had trials and sadness, but they also had the protection and peace from choosing the right.

We started learning the song, line by line, as I expertly wielded my shield.

Tip: When teaching songs, I will often have the kids repeat each line in different voices. For example, in my best angelic singing-voice I'll sing "I am a Child of God," and the kids will answer, repeating the line in their best angelic singing voice.

After a few lines, I gave everyone a half sheet of paper. I asked them what a shield is supposed to protect you from and then told them that my CTR shield helps protect me from bad choices. I then told them to choose a bad choice for their paper to represent. A few kids shared what their paper represented: lying, cheating, choosing the wrong, murder, "my brother shooting me", etc.

I then had them wad their papers into a ball and told them to hold the papers calmly because, if they sang well, we would do something fun with them.

After another line or two of the song, we tested my CTR shield. I specifically told them that my shield was so big because I'd been choosing the right a lot. They could throw all the trials they wanted at me and my CTR shield would help protect me. Then, on the count of three, all the kids threw their papers. A couple bad choices made their way through and hit me, which is a lesson in and of itself, but in general I was protected. I still experienced hardship, but it would have been worse without my shield.

Some kids will probably try and grab papers already thrown to be able to keep throwing. You can tell everyone to hurry and find a ball and return to their seats quickly so that the cycle of throwing doesn't take over your lesson.

After a few more lines of the song, I told them that my shield was heavy and it was too time consuming to choose the right so much. Could I only choose the right a little bit and get the same protection? Then, and I got a great reaction from this, I put away my big shield and pulled a tiny shield out of my purse. This shield was just big enough to fit inside my palm.

We sang a few more lines and then I told the kids to find a position in the room they thought would give them the best angle to throw at me. Be prepared for chaos and many papers to the face. My own kid went behind me, where I had no cover from the tiny shield! As they threw, I ninja-waved my tiny shield around, but I don't think it protected me much.

We sang the song in full and I pointed out that the large shield (choosing the right more often) gave me better protection. If they ever find themselves using a small shield or having no shield at all, getting a bigger shield is easier than they think. Just start choosing the right, push yourself to make good choices, and the protection and peace will come.

Scan the QR Code for further resources

Lesson: Primary Musical!

Purpose: Connect primary songs to principles in a scripture story. Pairs well with any song.

Materials:

- Whatever props you may want to use to help tell the story.

This is a fun activity that gives every kid plenty of opportunities to participate. All you need is a scripture story, a list of songs that might help the kids to learn about the story, and whatever props you can get your hands on.

When I did this lesson, we were learning about the twelve tribes of Israel and Joseph's time in Egypt. I wrote out the simplified story on a piece of paper and then wrote what songs we could sing as we got to each part of the story.

Think outside of the box when it comes to which songs to use. When I told the 30-second story of Joseph's brothers selling him into slavery, we sang a song about prayer because prayer can help us get through hard things.

Everyone got a chance to either come up and be one of the characters or use a prop. Look for places where you can use several volunteers at once. In this story, I had Jacob, Joseph, the 12 brothers, Pharaoh, the baker, the butler, guards, someone to hold the dream bubble (a picture that depicted what was being dreamt about), several kids to wave around light wands (for the dream about stars), etc. I own my own light wands, so I bring them whenever I can as a fun treat.

Use whatever props you want to help tell the story. The props can be as simple or as complex as you want. For the Joseph story, I brought a rainbow towel to use as the multi-colored coat. I also brought the light sticks, a couple of "staffs" for the guards, a toy rolling pin for the baker, a cup for the butler, pictures to represent the dreams, a cardboard necklace for the Pharaoh, and cardboard beards for Jacob and his twelve sons.

Want to do this idea but don't want to prepare props? Come up with a part for each class or row and give them three minutes at the beginning of singing time to color their own prop on a piece of paper. If you have four rows in your primary, and you were doing the story of Joseph, you could make one row color beards for the 12 brothers, one row color something to make them Egyptians (Pharaoh, Baker, Butler, Guards, etc.), one row to color stars (to represent Joseph's dreams), and one row to color cattle (to represent Pharaoh's dreams).

This is an easy way to review a bunch of songs and also learn about the scriptures.

Scan the QR code for further resources

Lesson: The Crown of a Child of God

Purpose: We can choose the right and recognize our blessings from being children of God

Pairs well with songs that discuss our heavenly heritage, service, and heavenly virtues.

Materials:

- Pieces of a large crown (see below)
- Tape

The purpose of this lesson is four-fold. 1) To remind the kids that they are children of God. 2) To help them understand what being a Child of God means. 3) To help them know what to do when they feel that their crown "falls off." 4) To help them learn that serving others is an important part of being a child of God.

In this lesson, you are building a crown fit for a child of God. It doesn't have to be fancy, mine was made with cardboard and paint. It started as a large, basic crown that I wore as the children came in. I wanted it to be huge so that the kids had something to gawk at and whisper about when they came in the room. Immediately, the crown was a spectacle.

I had made attachments that could be added to the crown, either by fitting it over another piece with slits in the cardboard or hanging it on top. Each attachment was labeled with a blessing we receive as children of God. For example, one attachment could be a picture of the scriptures. Another could have a picture of the sun on it with the words, "I can be a light and an example to others." I started the lesson by asking the kids if they liked my crown. My Heavenly Father is a king, so that makes me a princess, right? We then talked about how we are all princes and princesses as sons and daughters of God. I said, I'm not sure my crown is spectacular enough for a child of God. When I asked if anyone wanted to help me make it more spectacular, most kids raised their hands.

I told them that we were going to learn a song that teaches us something very important about being a child of God: Service. We learned the first line of our service-themed song, and then I asked for a volunteer to choose an attachment for my crown. I let them know that, even though we are children of God, sometimes there are going to be people or situations that try to make them forget who they are and knock off their crown. While that volunteer was choosing an attachment, I asked for another volunteer to choose an action that they think will knock my crown off.

Most actions were things such as jumping, spinning, marching, dancing, or a form of Simon Says where I followed what the kid was doing. I had the volunteer that chose the action, plus a couple of others, come up to help me lead the primary in the action.

After I put the first attachment on my crown, we sang the first line together while doing the action.

The rest of class continued in similar fashion. We would add one, two, or three attachments as we learned each new section or line of the song, and then the whole primary would participate in the actions with me. I would also give a super brief comment about each blessing attachment as I put it on my crown. For example, we talked about important blessings like temples, families, the Holy Ghost, and the Priesthood. This should be kept simple and quick so that the class can focus on the singing.

The kids all loved when my crown would grow taller. The squeals of delight and surprise, especially when it almost touched the ceiling, were infectious. When my crown would fall apart or off my head completely, they would laugh super loud.

It was a blast.

Each time it would fall apart, I would stop the primary with a loud theatrical voice, pause for effect and say, "It's OK! 'Cause you know what I do when my crown falls off? Fix it!" I then fix it and keep going. If there's ever a time that you don't act like a Child of God, you repent and keep following him.

At the end of the lesson, after we'd had sufficient fun with our shenanigans, I ended the lesson by telling them that Satan wants them to forget about the crown. He wants to knock it off. Sometimes you might say or do things that you may realize aren't how a child of God

should act. I ask: So what do you do when you feel sad because of a mistake and feel like your crown has fallen off?

Hopefully by this point they will respond in loud fashion: fix it! The idea that these heavy feelings can be fixed is an important concept. I ended the lesson there due to time. Most likely you won't have time to expound on how to fix it. However, singing songs such as "My Heavenly Father Loves Me" can teach the children about remembering that they are loved. Other songs, such as those that deal with topics such as repentance and service can help us come closer to God.

Scan the QR code for further resources

Lesson: Be Bold in Following Christ.

Purpose: We can follow Christ despite opposition.
Pairs well with songs that discuss choosing the right, following Christ, and being valiant.

Materials:

- Props that help recreate a scripture story in which someone boldly chooses the right (see below).

When I taught this lesson, I wanted to teach the kids about Moses' time in Egypt, as well as show the kids that we can boldly follow Christ, no matter the opposition. I would list an obstacle that Moses faced and then ask if he gave up. The kids would answer, "No!" Then we would sing a song that corresponded to the brave thing Moses was doing. For example, you could sing a song about prayer when discussing how Moses asked God for help.

This could work for any scripture story in which people are choosing the right.

With the Moses example, I had kids putting up signs of the different plagues all around the room while we sang songs about being bold and brave.

Lesson: I Can Build an Ark by Choosing the Right.

Purpose: We can build an ark of spiritual safety by making good choices.
Pairs well with songs that discuss Noah, prophets, and choosing the right.

Materials:

- Some kind of ark that is missing a roof
- A roof for the ark
- Little planks of paper with ways to choose the right on them

I've seen lots of different ways to recreate an ark for your primary class, everything from posters to wood blocks. I personally made a 3-D cardboard ark because I love creating that kind of thing. Choose whatever is best for you, whatever floats your boat (pun intended).

At the beginning of the lesson, I asked if the kids knew what I was holding. Most of the kids called out that it was an ark. I told them they were right, but there was something wrong with my boat. I then tipped it forward to show the top and exclaimed that the roof is missing. Anyone inside would get rained on!

I told them that we were going to build a roof for the ark. However, where Noah built the ark with wood, we were going to build our ark by choosing the right.

Note: Any time I say "choose the right," I say, "Choose the . . ." And the kids call back, "Right!"

As we learned the first verse to the song, I paused between lines to let multiple kids come up and pick a little "choose the right" paper plank to tape to a piece of cardboard we could use as the roof. I had several "trust in God" planks, because that is a big part of the story of Noah. I also made planks that said things like "be kind" and "pay tithing." I read some of these aloud as the kids taped them to the roof.

I made sure to remind them that even though Noah built his ark, the floods still came. Even when we choose the right, trials will still happen in our lives. Our "choose the right" arks will help us handle and get through those challenges.

At the end of the lesson we had learned the first verse (or most of the first verse in junior primary) and I put the roof on top of the ark so they could see the finished product.

Huzzah!

Scan the QR code for further resources

Lesson: Being Able to Choose the Right Is a Blessing.

Purpose: It is a blessing to be able to choose the right because of Christ's plan.
Pairs well with songs that discuss choosing the right and blessings.

Materials:

- A Christ's Plan puzzle
- A Satan's Plan puzzle

Satan's Plan Puzzle:

It's really easy to make a Satan's plan puzzle. You just need several (enough for most if not all the kids in your primary) squares of paper that are all the same size and color. I then put my squares of paper in a flat box (like a puzzle or pizza box). Like all puzzle boxes, I put the picture of what the finished puzzle is supposed to look like on the front of the box. In my case; a big, blue square.

This was the easiest thing to make since it was just a bunch of blue, square pieces of paper.

Christ's Plan Puzzle:

This was easy to make as well since I just took a picture of a temple out of a church magazine and cut it into squares. You could also use a picture of a family, church leaders, Christ, or whatever you have that might be a good representation of Christ's plan.

At the beginning of my lesson, I put on my excited face and told the kids we were going to do a puzzle while singing our songs. A few of them were excited, but most were just going along with it because there was nothing else to do.

I made sure to open my Satan's plan puzzle box and put it on the table at the front of the room. From their seats, no one could see the blue squares inside or the blue square on the top of the box.

Between singing songs and learning lines, I asked for volunteers to come up. I made a big deal about how there were so many options and cool puzzle pieces for the kid to choose from. The first kid to come up looked inside the box and got a funny look on their face. Because, well, blue squares. At my direction, the kid chose a piece and then put it on the board. After that, as kids came up, I would tell them to put these "awesome" pieces on the board where the kids thought they should go. I had up to four kids come up at a time while we sang.

Pretty quickly, a few kids called me out, saying that they didn't have a lot of options and the puzzle pieces were the same. I made a very theatrical show of looking at the blue squares on the board and acting like I'd never seen such art. I even had the kids practice oohing and aahing with me. Some kids thought the puzzle was about the sky or looked like a whale, but . . . no.

At one point, between singing, I acted concerned that the puzzle wasn't taking shape and told the kids we should check the picture on the box to see if we were doing it correctly. I loved holding up the box with the example blue square on the front, because I enjoy setting up that kind of reverent sarcasm. It got a chuckle out of some of the teachers, too.

About two thirds of the way into my lesson I threw a fit. This puzzle wasn't cool like I was told it would be! There are no options, every puzzle piece is the same! You can't even choose what puzzle piece you want because they are all blue and square. This puzzle is lame!

Some of the kids agreed, but most of them tried very sweetly to comfort me.

One kid in senior primary actually spoke up, saying the puzzle was like Satan's plan. I was floored, because I didn't have to say it myself. "This is totally like Satan's plan. He didn't want us to have a choice, either. His puzzle and plan are not only lame, but it doesn't lead to a beautiful picture. Having a choice is important because it leads to learning and making something great."

I then sighed and said that it would be much better if we could have a Christ's plan puzzle where our choices actually led to something wonderful. Then I whipped out the Christ's plan puzzle—acting surprised—and we kept singing while more kids came up to work together to finish Christ's puzzle, one piece at a time.

After the singing was over, I turned around to look at the picture of the temple. It was somewhat recognizable, but some sarcastic kids decided to place a few pieces in random spots across the room and way off to the side.

This mistake was perfect! I pointed to the somewhat correct part of the temple and reminded them that sometimes making good choices isn't easy, but we can keep the end goal in mind to help us. Then I pointed to one of the puzzle pieces across the board and said that sometimes it is very hard to make good choices, but you can always repent and get back on track.

Scan the QR code for further resources

Lesson: Faith Is like a Little Seed.

Purpose: Inspiration for testimonies can come in all sizes, both small and large.
Pairs well with songs that discuss faith.

Materials:

- A ruler
- Four folding chairs

This is an easy lesson that needs almost no prep. If you can find a ruler and four folding chairs, you'll be set.

We learned a song about faith, learning actions to go along with each line. For example, when the song talked about a sun rising, we held our arms above our heads in a circle. You could just as easily use pictures or other visual aids to help them learn the song. When we got to the line about faith being like a little seed, I asked the kids questions like, "Who has ever helped plant a seed?" I then asked them to show me how big the seeds they planted were. Of course, they all indicated very little seeds. I asked them to guess how big the biggest seed in the world is and to hold up their hands to show me their guess. I then went around with my ruler to see if anyone was close to the 12 inches of a Coco Del Mer Seed. I took a minute to tell them about the biggest seed in the world and remind them that sometimes the seeds that help grow our testimony are small and sometimes they are big.

As we learned the rest of the song, I would pause between lines to have kids come up and help me lift folding chairs. One average folding chair is a little heavier than a normal coconut, and four chairs is about the weight of a Coco Del Mer Seed. At first we lifted one chair, with four kids helping me out. Then we did two, which is half the weight of a Coco Del Mer. Then we did three chairs, and then finally four. The four chairs were much heavier of course, and at that point I had at least six kids up there helping me. In senior primary, I let a couple boys come up to see if they could lift the chairs in pairs or solo. This was slightly dangerous, since the song leader has to be in charge of making sure no one gets hurt, but the older boys loved the challenge. Tip: Show them how to hold the chairs so they don't squish their fingers or toes.

At the end of the lesson I reminded the children to watch for opportunities for small and large testimony seed experiences. Because whether you have a small seed (like admiring the world around us that Christ made) or a large seed (like getting a life-changing revelation), all faith seeds are important and can grow into a powerful testimony.

Lesson: Song Toolbox

Purpose: Church songs can be used to help comfort and strengthen us. Pairs well with any song.

Materials:

- A tool box
- Ribbon wands or handkerchiefs or something for the kids to wave
- Slips of paper with the songs you want to sing written on them

When I taught this lesson, I was hoping to impress upon the kids that the songs we had been learning could be used as tools. Songs could be used to comfort, remind, and help the kids make good choices. I taught this lesson on Halloween Sunday, so I wrote "fear not" on the board and then made a point of telling the kids that these songs could help us to not be afraid: that when we are scared or overwhelmed or sad, we can sing these songs to help us through.

I called on a reverent kid to come up and help me, letting them pick something out of my tool box. I had filled it with ribbon wands that my primary owns and taped the slips of paper with the songs onto each wand.

When a wand and song had been chosen, I gave a couple ideas of how that particular song could be used as a tool and then had the kid help lead the song by waving the wand. At the next song, I had the kid pass off their wand so someone who hadn't had a turn yet and then I chose another kid to come get another "tool" out of the box. Because the kids passed off their wand at the end of each song, we were able to give every kid at least one turn. This use of the turn snowball effect is a really great way to help everyone get involved.

Scan the QR code for further resources

Lesson: I Am like a Star.

Purpose: Each of us is important and needed in the kingdom of God. Pairs well with songs that discuss stars, individual worth, and children of God.

Materials:

- Light makers
- Star projector
- Christmas lights
- Black garbage bags

Note: This is a really big lesson with lots of parts. I gave this lesson during an hour where I was teaching the entire primary. You could easily break this down into several smaller lessons.

How to make a star projector:

There are lots of how-to videos online, but in the end I chose two ways to create star projectors that the kids could take turns using.

The first projector was made by painting a smallish cardboard box black and then poking holes in it with a screw driver. Then I filled the box with Christmas lights connected to an extension cord. The second projector was made by filling a metal canister with Christmas lights, connected to an extension cord, and then covering it with aluminum foil that has been poked with a screw driver. The problem with this projector is that it heated up really fast and we couldn't use it for very long at any one time.

The point of this lesson was to help the kids remember that they are each special and that they can each have their light shine. At first, we sang the songs we were working on while the kids took turns giving light shows by literally having their light shine (the star projectors).

Next, I brought out different kinds of light toys for them to take turns giving light shows while we sang. I had light wands and some rainbow light sticks. Depending on how many I had, some needed one volunteer at a time, while others needed several. I made comments about how we can shine our lights and be good missionaries and examples through the entire lesson.

Then I brought out a strand of Christmas lights with one of the bulbs removed, but I didn't tell the kids that I had removed the bulb. Before class, I had hidden the little bulb by the pianist in a place where it wouldn't get lost or stepped on or messed with. Of course, with one bulb missing, a whole section of the lights wouldn't turn on.

While other kids kept giving light shows, I had volunteers come up one at a time, usually an older kid, to see if they could figure out what was wrong with the lights and why a section wouldn't turn on. None of them could figure it out.

Make sure you think through what you might want to say ahead of time whether the first kid figures it out or none of them figure it out.

At the end of class, I picked up the pile of lights and, finding the one missing light, held the blank space up for all to see. I acted shocked, because I wanted to accentuate the fact that only one light is missing. Why would one missing light affect the whole strand? I then gave a kid a clue to where they could find the missing light and the kid searched for it, eventually bringing it to me.

This part of the lesson could have been a whole different primary singing time activity. We could have talked about missionary work and how Christ goes after the one sheep, while the kids searched for the lights during singing time.

I made a big show of screwing in the light and being amazed when the entire string of light started working. I said something like, "Wait a minute, wait a minute. So, one little light made that big of a difference? One little light was that important to the whole string of lights?"

I then bore my testimony that, like the lights, each of us may feel small, but we are individually important. At the beginning and the end of the lesson I told the kids that if Christ and Heavenly Father have the power to create and take care of entire universes, then they must have the power to create and know and love each one of us. I reminded them to let their light shine, be good examples, and always remember how important they are.

Scan the QR code for further resources

Lesson: Stand in Holy Places.

Purpose: Choosing the right can help us withstand hardships.
Pairs well with songs that discuss choosing the right, following Christ, and the iron rod.

Materials:

- A rain simulator (see below)
- An umbrella
- Pictures to decorate the umbrella. These should depict ways we can choose the right.

Rain Simulator:

Get creative with how you make your rain simulator. There is no right or wrong way to make this, it just depends on what materials you already have on hand. The point of the simulator is to show that unless we stand under the CTR umbrella we will continuously get wet.

My rain simulator used the following materials:

- A plastic toy man
- Two wire shelving units with legs so that they can stand independently
- A shallow tub
- Binder clips
- A large plastic storage bag with holes poked into the bottom
- Blue paper
- Scissors
- Water in a pitcher
- A small umbrella that I made with wax paper and a straw. I super glued the umbrella to the top of a jar lid so that it would stand on its own, then I made a small CTR sign to tape to the straw, under the wax paper umbrella top. The wax paper made the umbrella waterproof. The umbrella was just big enough for the plastic toy man to stand under and be protected.
- Multiple small cups

To assemble the rain simulator, I put one of the wire shelves into the shallow tub. This shelving unit is where I put my small umbrella. Then, the other shelving unit went up on its end so that one of the sets of legs was hanging high over the CTR Umbrella.

Next, I made the "cloud." I took a large plastic bag and poked holes into the bottom. I tested to make sure the holes produced what looked like rain when water was poured into the bag. Then, I took some blue paper and cut out a cloud shape. That was easily attached to the bag with the binder clips, then those same binder clips clipped the bag to the legs of the shelving unit that were hanging over the umbrella. I was able to clip the bag so that the top stayed open a bit.

When I filled up the small cups with water from the pitcher and poured the cups into the plastic bag, it really did look like the cloud was raining. It took a bit of testing and adjusting to get the holes on the bag just right, but in the end it turned out fantastic!

For this lesson, I wanted the kids to learn that choosing the right and standing in holy places will help protect them from temptation and will help them withstand trials. I wanted them to see that, without the CTR umbrella, there was no chance that the plastic man wouldn't get soaked.

Between singing songs, I had one to three kids come up to the front of the room to pour water into the cloud. Each time I would tell the primary that we need to find a place where the man wouldn't get soaked by the rain. As part of this, after every song I would move the plastic man to a different place in the rain simulator. Basically, he could go anywhere but under the umbrella. I moved him all around the little shelf he was on, under the shelf, around the shallow tub, and I even put him in the rain cloud once.

Of course the kids got frustrated that I wasn't putting the little man under the umbrella, because that seems like the obvious solution. When they'd get after me, I'd say something like, "Wait, wait, wait. So you're telling me that if I just placed the man underneath the CTR umbrella, he'd be dry?" The kids would yell at me, letting me know that is the most obvious solution. So then I'd say something like, "Wait, wait, wait. So you're telling me that if we choose the right it will help protect us from the storms of temptation?" Then I'd think about it for a second and be like, "I don't know, let's keep trying other things first."

This made the kids frustrated, because of course the little man would be safer under the umbrella.

If this all seems a little on the nose, it's because it is. There is nothing wrong with pointing the kids in the right direction and then letting them stew on it for a while. This way, I tell them exactly what I want them to get out of the lesson, but they end up being the ones to champion the idea instead of me. By the end of the lesson, I had the kids trying to convince me to let the man stand under the CTR umbrella to protect him.

At the end of the lesson, I finally put the man under the umbrella and we tried the simulator again. This time, by standing under the Choose the Right umbrella, the man was protected. I pointed out to the kids that he may still get wet because it is still raining. Choosing the right doesn't take away the storms of life. We'll still get temptations and trials. Just because you choose the right, doesn't mean you won't have trials. But choosing the right will help you withstand those temptations and survive the hardships.

If you find yourself drenched in the rains of trials, it's never too late to get under the CTR umbrella.

Now, I knew I wouldn't get all of the kids up for a turn with the rain simulator. There just wouldn't be time for everyone to help. So I came up with a second way for the kids to help while we were singing. One to three kids would come up at a time and choose a picture from off the board. These pictures represented ways that we can choose the right and stand in holy places. Some examples are: going to the temple, giving service, going to church, paying tithing, etc.

The kids that chose a picture got to tape it to the outside of the umbrella. In doing this, we made a visual representation of our "CTR umbrella" that can help protect us from temptation. I still gave as many kids a turn with the simulator at a time as I could, because that's what everyone wanted to help with in the lesson.

When the kids first walked into the primary room, I had an actual umbrella open and over me, as if it was raining. This was a fun way to set the scene for the lesson. I know you aren't supposed to have an umbrella open inside, but . . . I did. As the prelude music was playing, I would walk around the room and hold out my hand from under the umbrella, acting like I was checking to see if it is raining. I would also rush over to kids and cover them with the umbrella, like it was pouring inside.

Some of the kids, particularly the older boys, were very indignant that it was not raining in the classroom. To those boys I'd point out that it is always raining. It was a way to foreshadow the lesson.

I got lots of positive feedback from this lesson. It took a little more work than most other lessons, but it was totally worth it.

Scan the QR code for further resources

Lesson: We Can Get Blessings from Our Trials.

Purpose: Trials, or how we view our trials, can turn into blessings. Pairs well with songs that discuss blessings, attitude, hope, and endurance.

Materials:

- Brown paper sacks
- Tiny squares of paper with green smiley faces on them. Have enough for all of the kids in the primary to have one, though they won't be given these
- Tiny squares of paper with red frowny faces on them (needs to be the same size as the smiley face papers). Have enough for all of the kids in the primary to have one.
- A bowl

I love using magic tricks in my lessons, and this was a great one!

I start by telling the kids that we can turn our trials into blessings. Throughout the class, in between songs, you can list ways for how you do that and why you do that.

The magic trick is actually pretty simple. You take two brown paper lunch sacks of the same size and cut an inch or two off of the top of one of them. Then you put a green smiley face paper in the bottom of the uncut bag.

Next, you place the cut bag into the uncut bag and line up the tops so that they are flesh with another. This creates a small space between the bags where the green smiley face sits. Then you roll down the tops of the bags to blend them together and make them look like one, wrinkled bag. When you look in the top, it appears empty.

Now all you need is a kid to place a red frowny face into the top. I like to ask the kids to name a trial, any trial, that the red frowny face could represent. Then, when the kid is sitting back in their chair, I ask the kids to count to three. As they count I blow air into the bag and on three I pop the bag. The kids love the pop!

Your magic trick is now complete. Popping the bags should create a tear in the bottom where then you can pull out the happy face or watch as it flutters to the floor.

The kids were amazed! You can talk about what sorts of blessings come from trials at this point.

Every single kid can participate in this lesson easily. As we sang our songs, I walked around the room with my prepped bag in one hand and a bowl full of frowny faces in the other. I gave each and every kid a turn to pick a frown and place it in the bag.

You do need to think about how many kids you are going to want to help with each bag so that you can pre-fill (at home) the smiley faces accordingly. If you have twenty frowns going in, no one is going to notice if only fifteen smileys come out. However, having an approximate number in each bag will help the trick come to life.

The older boys guessed at how the trick worked, but it didn't really matter. At that point they were interested and engrossed and that's all I really cared about.

Practice this one ahead of time, and be prepared for what to do if the lesson or magic trick goes south. What will you say if the frowns fall out instead of the smiles? You could mention that, while this is just a funny trick to help us picture the lesson, in real life it would have worked out. Or you could mention that sometimes, when we are trying to turn our trials into blessings, it takes us a bit to figure out how to do it.

At one point I popped the bag and, when I looked down at the magic trick, found that the inner bag had popped also! A ton of little red frowny faces were staring up at me with their devious eyes. Luckily, since I was standing, none of the kids in the room noticed. They couldn't see the mistake. So I grabbed out the stack of green smiles and then crumpled the rest of it up into a ball to hide the frowns. It was a close call and I seriously felt like angels had helped my lesson not fall apart. However, if the lesson does go south, use that as part of what you are trying to teach. Take the accident in stride and roll with it by using it as a chance to remind them that in real life you may have to work at this to be successful. If at first you don't succeed, try again.

I brought several bags prepped to do this project several times while we sang.

You don't have to have everyone go at once with this, they can take turns.

The kids loved the little green smiley faces falling out of the bag. In junior, a bunch of little kids ran up to the front when it rained smileys and started gathering them up to keep. Kids are sweet and will appreciate the "magic."

Scan the QR code for further resources

Lesson: Missionary Briefcase

Purpose: Every kid can become a good missionary.
Pairs well with songs that discuss missionaries and teaching the gospel.

Materials:

- A whiteboard
- Dry erase markers

For this lesson, I wanted the kids to realize that their own talents and choices can help them prepare to serve a mission and be a missionary now. This lesson is super easy and extremely low prep, so you can literally teach it at the last minute.

I started by drawing a big square around the outside of the whiteboard and then drawing a little handle on the top. I told the kids that this was my figurative missionary brief case, and that we were going to fill it with ways we could be a missionary. Between singing each song, I asked if anyone had a skill or talent that could help them share the gospel or to be a good example. I gave them tips, like reminding them that everything from being a good friend to learning to play an instrument, to participating in sports can help them be a good example.

When a kid told me their skill, I asked if they wanted to come draw it on the board, inside the brief case. I then asked if any other kids, dependent on the number of markers I had, wanted to come up and draw their skill too. Sometimes I left it open-ended, and other times I made the request specific. Like, if someone said they can be a good example to their soccer team, I asked if anyone else wanted to come up and specifically draw something related to being a good missionary on a sports team.

The kids like to draw, so lessons like this are easy.

From my Auto-Husband 3000 lesson, I already had a life-size man with a dry erase face (see page 80). By adding a badge and tie, my cardboard man became a missionary. So, between each song, I also called on a kid to come up and design his face. Everyone likes to draw on the face and this is always a hit.

Scan the QR code for further resources

Lesson: We Are Part of God's Army.

Purpose: We can stand with God no matter what obstacles are in our way.
Pairs well with songs that discuss choosing the right, trials, being valiant, following God and Christ, and strength.

Materials:

- A small obstacle course
- Small CTR shield
- Optional: Big CTR shield and other armor

I wanted the kids to always remember that we can stand for what is right at all times, against all foes and despite all obstacles, because we are in God's army.

Before class started, I set up a little obstacle course at the front of the room. It was very simple, made with things I already had. The kids would jump over a rectangle of tape on the floor, weave through orange cones, go under a PVC pipe structure, run around a chair, and then hold up a small CTR shield while saying something like, "Bam!"

I wanted them to wield that shield with power.

When they entered the room, I welcomed them while holding my large CTR shield and sword of truth that I had from other lessons. Having these props is extra, but I use them whenever I can. I started the lesson by reminding them that we are all in God's army and we can stand for what is right no matter what obstacles get in our way.

As we learned our song, different kids got a turn to see how fast they could go through the course. Because I wanted everyone to have a turn, I had multiple people go at a time, one right after another. At the end, I had anyone who hadn't had a turn line up at the side of the room and go in quick succession. When more than one person was going through the course, I moved the CTR shield and had them hold their arms up to show their strong muscles. Some of the older kids weren't too thrilled about that, but we made a game of it. I hope they at least remember that they are strong.

Scan the QR code for further resources

Lesson: Pioneers Worked Hard and Played Hard.

Purpose: We can learn from the Pioneer's hope and work ethic. Pairs well with songs that discuss pioneers.

Materials:

- A fake fire
- Blankets for the kids to sit on
- Materials for pioneer activities

I got the basic idea for this from a social media group I follow. There were lots of music leaders who were going to make a fake fire in the middle of the room and then have the kids sit around it while singing. I loved this idea because it is very hands on learning, but I decided to make a few adjustments. Mainly, I wanted to tell a couple of pioneer stories while having us sing pioneer-themed songs and do pioneer-themed activities.

This is a lot to do in such a short amount of time, but it worked out. I dressed up in pioneer garb and pretended like we had all just ended a day of walking across the plains. I even had the kids sing a song about walking and speed walk in place so that we were plum tired. I made a comment or two about why the pioneers were crossing the plains so that the kids kept in mind why we are studying this.

I told them that at the end of a long day the pioneers gathered together and did chores. The pioneers worked very hard!

Then I orchestrated the following activities:

- Some kids found sticks hidden around the room to add to the fire while we sang a song.
- Some kids gathered up paper cows from around the room while we sang a song.
- Some kids then lassoed the cows while we sang.
- One kid found the hidden buffalo (to stand for food) while we sang.
- Everyone got a graham cracker (in place of pioneer hard tack) while I told one of my favorite pioneer stories.

When appropriate, I shared a quick pioneer story to make the activities real. I know that some leaders will have the kids make butter, do a potato bag race, make or play with pioneer toys, etc.

I told them that some pioneers were able to bring their instruments, like fiddles, with them across the plains. And sometimes, at the end of a long day, the pioneers would dance. I had everyone stand and do their best pioneer jig or clap their hands or stomp their feet. I am lucky to be a fiddler myself, and I played one of the pioneer songs with a fiddling edge.

At the end of the lesson, I bore my testimony about how God guides us and how grateful I am for such an amazing heritage.

Scan the QR code for further resources

Lesson: The Holy Ghost Speaks to Us in Different Ways.

Purpose: We can learn how the Holy Ghost speaks to us as individuals.
Pairs well with songs that discuss the Holy Ghost and revelation.

Materials:

- None

This is another lesson that requires little to no preparation. I started out by telling the kids that the Holy Ghost speaks to everyone in different ways and that it is our job to figure out how He speaks to us. We can practice hearing the Spirit and over time our ability to hear Him will increase. It is a life-long endeavor.

Then, as we learned our song line by line, I asked for kids to name different ways the Holy Ghost can talk to us. Eventually, when no one could think of any more, I shared an example from a list I made ahead of time. Then I asked for someone to come up with an action to represent that way He talks to us. For example, for sends us thoughts, a kid suggested pointing to their head. Another kid said that the Holy Ghost could help us picture something and we all took air photos. We would then sing the song up to that point or just sing the next line while doing that action.

The only preparation I had to do for this lesson was make a list of different ways the Holy Ghost speaks to us so that I had a reference list for ease.

At the end of the lesson, I shared a personal experience of when the Holy Ghost spoke to me in a seemingly odd way.

Lesson: Tell a Story

Purpose: Some songs are sung as a story.
Pairs well with any song that is sung as a story.

Materials:

- Pictures that go along with every line of the song

When teaching a song that is sung in story format, consider letting the children practice their storytelling skills. This is a great opportunity to talk about the importance of the story you are learning and why we sing about it. For example, one of my favorite songs teaches us about Joseph Smith's experience in the grove. When we sing this song, we learn about the First Vision and we remember that Heavenly Father knows us by name, that He has a plan for us, and that He answers our prayers (even if it isn't how we want them answered).

Have kids come up to the front and hold the pictures as you learn each line. The pictures will help them learn the song. When you get at least three pictures up, if not five or six, have the kids go give their pictures to someone else and then see if the new kids can figure out the right order in which to stand. Keep singing, adding pictures while you learn new lines, and then mixing the pictures up again.

Scan the QR code for further resources

Lesson: Following

Purpose: We can follow Jesus Christ and the prophet.
Pairs well with songs that discuss following Christ and the prophet, being a child of God, choosing the right, and the commandments.

Materials:

- Something to follow

This is a very simple lesson that can be thrown together with literally no preparation. After a thirty second introduction where I reminded the children of the importance of following Christ or following the prophet, depending on what song we were singing that day, I then told the children we were going to test their following skills while learning our song.

While learning the lines of the song, I have the children play follow the leader. One day I let the children choose which poses or actions we could do while singing the song (standing on one foot, leaning from side to side, hopping, or spinning). During another lesson, we took turns using ribbons and let the kids follow each other's ribbon spinning routines.

Scan the QR code for further resources

Lesson: He Lives.

Purpose: The tomb is empty because Christ lives.
Pairs well with songs that discuss Christ and the atonement.

Materials:

- Empty tomb
- Pictures of Christ, each with a different line of the song on the back
- Period clothing

There are lots of different ways you can do this same lesson, but my main goal was to teach the kids that "Christ Lives" is not just about an empty tomb. It's talking about how Christ is actively trying to guide and help us. He lived then and He lives now.

A few years ago, my mom and I were teaching a primary class as part of our participation in the pilot for *Come, Follow Me*. We decided to make an empty tomb out of gray sheets and paint. We then hung the sheets on a roll-around garment rack. We have used this tomb multiple times for church classes and family Easter events.

For this particular lesson, you don't need something as intricate as our tomb. You could just make a chalk drawing or a poster of an empty tomb. You could also take an empty box and cut a door in the side. It doesn't really matter what kind of empty tomb you have.

The basic idea is that the kids can take turns pulling out a picture of Christ from the tomb (I used pictures cut from church magazines). The picture then gets placed on the board in a collage while you teach the next line of the song, the line that was on the back of the picture. In order to do this, the pictures/lines have to be in order in the tomb.

As part of my mission to make sure every kid gets a turn, I always chose two volunteers. One chose the next picture out of the tomb and the other chose where the picture went in the collage. Any kids who didn't get a turn during the lesson got to have a quick turn either taking out a picture or placing it on the board while we sang the song one last time.

For fun, I dressed up in a long dress with a curtain panel around my shoulders and a table cloth over my head, trying to look like I was from the time of Christ. When music time started, I said something like:

"I'd like to tell you a little about me. I come from the time when Jesus lived. Three days ago, he died on the cross after suffering for our sins in the Garden of Gethsemane. But now, Christ has just been resurrected. What does it mean to be resurrected?" After listening to answers, I'd continue. "It means He was reunited with his body and He will live forever. And, because He conquered death, it means that we have the opportunity to choose the right and go back to live forever with our Heavenly Father as well. So I have a question. If Christ is alive in my day, is He alive in yours?"

Yes.

"But saying that our Savior, Redeemer, and Brother lives isn't just talking about an empty tomb. It's talking about how He is actively helping us, leading us, and supporting us. No matter what time you live in. Today we are going to sing a song that helps us know how He lives and helps us."

Lesson: The Auto-Husband 3000 (Father's Day)

Purpose: Good choices help men to be good husbands and fathers.
Pairs well with any church song.

Materials:

- A generic cardboard cut-out or poster of a man
- Pictures depicting qualities that help someone be a good father
- Accessories for each quality depicted

I wanted to do something different and fun for Father's Day that sticks with my goal to always teach a hands-on lesson. Since I am single, the answer was clear: The Auto-Husband 3000! It's a machine that helps me create a husband.

If you aren't single, then make an Auto-Dad 3000. For Mother's Day, you could make this an Auto-Wife or Auto-Mom 3000.

I started with something like, "For this Father's Day, I thought we'd talk about some of the qualities and attributes that helps someone be a good dad and husband. And how better to do that than with the Auto-Husband 3000? We're going to make me a Husband."

Cue snickers, mostly from the adults in the room.

The idea is that every quality or attribute picture has a song and accessory with it. I had a kid come up and choose an attribute picture, for example one that depicted kindness. Then we would put the accessories that went along with kindness on the cardboard husband and sing the song about it. And then I would say something like, "Does being kind help someone be a good dad? Yes!"

In the case of kindness, I chose a song that talked about being kind to others and walking with those in need. The accompanying accessory was the foot. I literally added a foot to the cardboard guy so he could "walk with you."

At the end of the lesson, you'll have reviewed lots of songs and decorated a husband.

I also made a dry-erase face with laminated paper. Some kids got to take turns drawing faces for my husband. This part of the activity was a hit!

Scan the QR code for further resources

Lesson: The Magic of Repentance

Purpose: Through the atonement of Christ we can repent and become clean.
This lesson pairs well with songs that discuss repentance, forgiveness, and the atonement.

Materials:

- A "magic" repentance envelope

For this lesson, I wanted to show the kids how we can repent and become clean from sin through the atonement of Christ.

In addition to making pictures to hang on the board and help us learn the song, I made a "repentance" envelope. The magic of the repentance envelope (one with a big plastic window in the front) is that when the envelope/frame is empty, it shows an image with a sad, tear-filled face and the words: Bad Choices. When a special picture is slid into the envelope and viewed through the plastic window, the image shows a happy face and the words: Good Choices.

You make the picture by drawing a happy face for choosing the right on a piece of hard, see-through plastic that then you attach to a piece of white paper. You only attach one side so that on the other you can separate the plastic and paper again. On the white paper you add details that, when combined with the plastic, make the smiley face look sad. The envelope works by being split in two: a front pocket and a back pocket. The kids can't see that there is a back pocket, but when you slide in the picture you are separating the plastic from the paper. This makes the sad details you added go into the hidden, back pocket, while the happy details can be seen from the front pocket.

Make sure you practice the magic trick, so that you are able to pull it off in front of the primary. When I did this, my envelope broke right as I was trying to show them! I had to ask someone to lead the primary in the song while I ducked into the hallway and fixed the envelope. When I walked back in, I turned my accident into positive by reminding the primary that repentance doesn't always go as planned. It's something you have to constantly work for.

Then, after we learned the chorus, I did the magic trick for them. The kids were amazed! A few of them thought they knew how I did it but, when they asked me for specifics, I told them it was repentance. Then I put the envelope up on the board with magnets and after each line we learned I pushed the picture in just a smidge. That way the kids could see the magic of repentance in slow motion.

Scan the QR code for further resources

Lesson: Breaking Down a Song.

Purpose: We can gain a deep understanding of each song.
Pairs well with any song.

Materials:

- Chalk and/or printed words
- Pictures

Every once in a while, I will break down a song for the primary, especially if it has a lot of confusing words and concepts in it. Sometimes I'll include another activity, but that depends on how much time I have. I usually go line by line, having the children repeat it and explaining what the line means.

If there is an emotion or action in the line, I have the children show it. If the line discussed happiness, I ask the children to show their best happy face. Or if the line talks about surprise, I have the kids show me their best surprised face.

This sort of plan is a good example of a reverent lesson. I personally tend to do a lot of active, borderline rowdy lesson plans, so I go out of my way to sandwich particularly crazy weeks with more calm, reverent weeks.

One week, I taught the kids the song "I Stand All Amazed". I had written out the lines I wanted to teach so that I could simply stick them up on the board. This particular song is about our relationship with the Savior. The first verse in particular is in a me-him format, so that each sentence can be split in half to show my part and his part.

Me: I stand all amazed. . . Him: at the love Jesus offers me.

If you make the "me" sections a different color than the "him" sections, it will help the kids see the relationship between us and Christ that this song highlights.

Some personal notes for the first verse of this song

- "Stand" can mean to actually stand, to support Christ, endure, etc. It means that, because of Christ's sacrifice, we are able to endure hardships and stand with him. For fun, have the kids stand up and sit down as slow or as fast as you direct them. Talk about what "amazed" means, and have the kids show their best "amazed" faces.
- Ask the kids, "What love does Jesus offer me?"
- Talk about what "confused" means, and have the kids show their best "confused" faces. You can see if the kids can go quickly back and forth between confused and amazed faces.
- Look up "grace" in the topics section of the church website and teach what this means. Specifically look at how it applies to the help given through His atonement.
- Talk about what "fully" means.
- A whole lesson could be given on the word "proffer." Why would the author add a "pr" to "offer?" What's the point? Look it up before you teach, but the short answer is that a proffer is an offer made ahead of the official discussions. In this case, it's an offer made before the time of judgment comes. So Christ offers his love, always. And he proffers his grace, before we really need it. We can rely on him and trust in him.

- Have the kids show their best "tremble." Remember that you can tremble for many reasons, including being amazed down to your core so that you tremble with gratitude and wonder.
- Ask what it means to be "crucified."
- This song points "me" out as a "sinner" and then immediately says "He suffered." In other words, He knows me, who I have been, who I am, and who I will be, and he still chose to suffer on my behalf. I am not perfect, but he loves me.
- For the chorus, I had them pump their hands over their hearts every time we sing "wonderful" or something he does for us. I told them this is to remind them that He loves them and that's what the song is about.

In my opinion, the key to this song and why Jesus chose to suffer for us can be found in the second verse. We are sufficient (in other words enough) for Jesus to want to own (make us His or bring us into His flock), to redeem, and to justify. We are enough. We are special. We are important.

I put this line on the back of a sheet and drew a key on the front. After we learned the first verse of the song and had been speaking of our relationship with Christ, I showed them the key and we talked about why Christ died for us. Because He loves us.

Scan the QR code for further resources

Lesson: Am I a Child of God?

Purpose: We are all children of God.
Pairs well with songs that discuss being a child of God.

Materials:

- A picture of you when you were a primary kid

When kids are in junior primary, they are always so excited to sing "I am a Child of God". It's a song they generally know pretty well and it's simple. But then there's something about senior primary that makes this song come out in bored, monotone words.

I tell my senior primary that they are literally children of God. That they come from a royal heritage, so why are they singing about it in such a bored voice?

This lesson can be done as quickly or as slowly as you need, but the end goal is to remind each kid that he or she is a son or daughter of God, no matter their age.

I recounted the shortened story found in Moses 1. Heavenly Father tells Moses that Moses is God's son. Then, when Satan comes tempting, Satan calls Moses a son of Man. And what was Moses's reaction? He asks Satan: "Who art thou?" Moses knows his personal, royal heritage. Do you?

You can ask: Am I a child of God? At my age? What if I was seventeen? What if I was one hundred and seven? What if I was one thousand and seven? Show the picture of you when you were a young child.

You can have your kids (and the adults) raise their hands if they are children of God.

Tip: This should all be done very quickly, as this is singing time, not talking time.

Now, sing "I am a Child of God".

You can expand on it and teach what each line means, or you can sing other related songs, such as "I Lived in Heaven".

When I taught this lesson, I wanted it to be a get-to-know-you activity. So, we took turns as different children of God shared their favorite primary song for us to sing.

Lesson: Don't forget to pray.

Purpose: Heavenly Father is just a prayer away
Pairs well with songs that discuss prayer, scripture study, and Heavenly Father.

Materials:

- A box
- A picture of Heavenly Father
- Paper
- Pen

This is one of my favorite lessons. Since it requires very little prep, this is a fun experience that you can pull off quickly.

Write various actions on pieces of paper. For example: do a dance, jumping jacks, run in circles, or balance on one foot. You are going to put these papers upside down in a place where the kids can take turns choosing from them. Other than that, you simply put a picture of Heavenly Father under a box at the front of the primary room. As kids walk in, they will surely be curious about what is under your box, but don't let them peek.

When you are ready for singing time, you say something along these lines:

"There is something under my box! A picture of something very special to me. Would you all like to see what it is? Great. Let's try some things to help us get inside this box."

As you sing or learn the songs you chose for the day, keep pausing to let volunteers come up and choose a paper. Whatever the paper says, have the kids do that action with you to see if it will help uncover what is under the box. For example, if the paper says "balance on one foot," have all the kids do it at the same time and then look expectantly at the box, pausing for effect. Make sure to act disappointed when nothing happens.

The kids will start out a bit confused, unsure of why you are thinking these random actions will help you see under the box. Pretty quickly, the kids are going to get frustrated because what you are doing makes no sense. I am sure you will quickly hear, "Just lift up the box!"

At which point I would say something like, "What? No . . . are you sure? Let's keep trying some of these other ideas first."

By the end of class, you are going to have the kids all sorts of frustrated with you. And of course, you still won't have revealed what's under your box. This is when you ask if maybe you should just, I don't know, try lifting up the box.

Be prepared for the kids to throw a fit, because this is exactly what they have been begging you to do for all of class.

You can ask for guesses as to what picture is underneath, and then get a volunteer or two to help you lift up the box.

At this point, I expressed to the class how I wished I had just lifted up the box in the first place. "Wasn't it silly?" I asked them. "Wasn't it silly that I tried to do all those other things instead of something so simple as lifting up the box? I could have saved myself a lot of trouble by simply picking it up."

I then told them that, although this seems silly, people do this all the time in real life. Instead of simply getting on their knees and praying to Heavenly Father, sometimes people forget to pray. They forget that they have an easy, ever-present line of communication to God to thank him for his blessings and ask for his help in times of need.

"So, when you need His help, remember to pray. Don't dance around a box when you could just lift it up."

Scan the QR code for further resources

Acknowledgments

A HUGE THANK YOU TO MY MOM FOR BEING MY BIGGEST SUPPORTER. For listening to all my lesson and book ideas. For putting me through years of music lessons. For being my rock through hard times. I will never be able to express my full gratitude to you.

To my daughter, you are the sunshine in my life, the best thing about me, and my favorite beta reader. Just between the two of us, you were and always will be my favorite music student.

A heartfelt thank you to the angels at Cedar Fort Publishing. You all have made my dream come true.

Thank you to my grandparents, who loved my music. I loved your music, too.

Thank you to all my beta readers, past and present and those who have supported me along my journey. To my aunt who always asks to read and to the friends that keep asking where the next installments of my fiction books are. Thank you to my friends at the American Night Writers Association and all my author friends. And thank you to all my music teachers, I promise I never lied on my practice charts.

Thanks to everyone I've worked with in both stake and ward primary and music callings who have taught and helped me so much. All the leaders, teachers, and children have been an immense blessing in my life.

Even if you are not vaguely named here, I appreciate all who have helped and supported me.

And last but always first, thank you to my Lord and Savior Jesus Christ. This book is about you.

About the Author

Jenelle Allred is a long-time music teacher and primary music enthusiast. She firmly believes that there is a hymn to help with every trial and heartbreak. Learning those hymns starts in Primary.